ALASKA WILDLIFE CONSERVATION CENTER

by Doug Lindstrand

The primary concern of the Alaska
Wildlife Conservation Center (AWCC) is
the preservation of Alaska's native wildlife.

©2006 Douglas W. Lindstrand
ISBN: 1-928722-03-2

Publisher: Sourdough Studio
Computer layout: Mary Humphrey
Printed in Korea
Printing and binding through
    AIPEX.com Seattle, WA.
First U.S. Edition: April, 2006

Contact Information:

  Alaska Wildlife Conservation Center
PO Box 949
Mile 79 Seward Highway
Portage Glacier, Alaska 99587-0949
Phone: (907) 783-2025
Toll-Free: (866) 773-2025
Fax: (907) 783-2370
Web site: www.alaskawildlife.org
E-mail: info@alaskawildlife.org

AWCC Bull moose

Cover: Grizzly bears at play.
Page 1: Muskox calf.

Doug photographing along Turnagain Arm.

Author's comments: Doug Lindstrand has been a free-lance artist and photographer ever since arriving in Alaska via a tour in Vietnam. "AWCC is one of my favorite Alaska places", Doug said, "as it gives me an opportunity to watch, study and record the Center's magnificent animals throughout the year. For years I have witnessed the dedicated staff and volunteers of AWCC work tirelessly caring for the countless injured and orphaned wildlife creatures brought to the facility. I urge visitors to consider becoming Members to help support the mission of this exemplary organization. Please contact AWCC through the above "Contact Information" for details on joining. Thank you".

Books by Doug Lindstrand: Wild Alaska, Mountain Royalty, Alaska Sketchbook, Drawing America's Wildlife, Drawing Big Game, The Artist's Guide to Drawing Realistic Animals, Drawing Mammals, Deer: the Ultimate Artist's Reference, and Bear: the Ultimate Artist's Reference.

www.douglindstrand.com

AWCC's mission is to:

- Provide refuge for orphaned, injured and ill animals.
- Take care of animals that cannot survive in the wild.
- Educate visitors about Alaska's wildlife.

We provide an opportunity for Alaska residents and visitors to view wildlife in a scenic setting. We strive to establish a natural habitat for each species.

Elk calves running and playing in their spacious AWCC pasture.

The Alaska Wildlife Conservation Center (AWCC) is a 200 acre non-profit conservation, education, and recreation facility dedicated to the care of orphaned, injured, and displaced native Alaskan wildlife. AWCC is open everyday, year-round.

Located at the southern edge of Turnagain Arm and the entrance to the Portage Valley, AWCC provides superior care and spacious habitats for indigenous Alaskan animals that cannot survive in the wild.

AWCC is a 501 (c) (3) non-profit organization. All proceeds from admission, gift and food sales are dedicated to the animals in our care and AWCC's education programs.

BALD EAGLE: Adonis is a gunshot victim found near a remote village in Alaska. His wing required full amputation. He has lived at AWCC since 1995.

Table Of Contents

Flowers at AWCC

Tidelands at AWCC

POSITION STATEMENT

The Alaska Wildlife Conservation Center believes that the survival of our native wildlife should be a matter of grave concern to all of us. Wild creatures and the wild places they inhabit are not only an abiding source of wonder and inspiration but are an integral part of our future well being.

HISTORY

Founded by Mike Miller in 1989, the Alaska Wildlife Conservation Center (AWCC) opened to the public in 1993. AWCC originally operated under the name of Big Game Alaska, Inc. with a modest herd of Plains bison and Rocky Mountain elk. In 2000, Big Game Alaska, Inc. received its non-profit status and formally changed its name to the Alaska Wildlife Conservation Center to better reflect its intended purpose and mission.

Over the last decade, AWCC has grown, expanding its wildlife exhibits to include over 80 animals in 15 habitats. Its ample acreage allows it room to expand its future exhibits.

Coyotes in winter coats. AWCC's family of coyotes share an 18-acre enclosure with grizzly bears.

AWCC works closely with state and federal agencies to provide year-round wildlife emergency treatment and rehabilitation strategies. The Center's public education offerings utilize naturalist guides trained to deliver wildlife education programs concentrating on Alaska's native species. AWCC's exhibits include Wood and Plains bison, moose, elk, caribou, black and grizzly bears, musk-ox, Sitka Black-tailed deer, lynx, coyotes, foxes, and birds of prey. Special attention is given to each exhibit to maintain the natural habitat of each species.

Hugo, who is perhaps the most playful grizzly that this book's author has ever seen, tosses and plays with a hooligan. Hooligan are a small, oily, smelt-like fish that migrates up the area's streams during the spring. Also, the streams that border AWCC also host summer runs of spawning salmon.

Antlers are shed yearly by members of the deer family such as deer, elk, caribou, and moose. A variety of antlers are displayed here at the lodge.

PARTNERSHIPS

Recognizing the importance of interagency relationships, the AWCC maintains continuing partnerships with the U.S. Fish & Wildlife Service, Alaska Department of Fish and Game, USDA Forest Service and USDA Natural Resource Conservation Service.

Bull elk (shedding last remnants of their antler's "velvet")

A well-maintained road with ample room to accommodate large tour buses and motor homes provides access to AWCC wildlife habitats. A beautifully crafted hand-hewn lodge, constructed from a harvest of local beetle-killed spruce, houses the Center's gift shop. During summer months, the lodge deck houses the Center's snack bar. A covered observation platform offers unobstructed views of the Center's moose habitat and shelter for visitors during inclement weather. The Center's network of roads accommodates habitat observation for tour buses and other vehicles.

School groups are frequent visitors to AWCC and are given guided tours by naturalists. These educational tours help introduce Alaska's wildlife to these young people and teaches them about our responsibility of protecting their environment and the animal's habitats.

AWCC'S SAFETY GUIDELINES

1. Keep all children away from fences.
2. Do not pet or hand-feed any animals.
3. Help keep our grounds beautiful. Please leave all plants and flowers for the enjoyment of others.
4. Put garbage in its proper place. Litter is a deadly hazard to animals.
5. Keep pets in vehicle at all times.
6. Please respect the animals and refrain from taunting or harassing them.

** Please remember that some of the fences here at AWCC have electric wires running along them for protection. However, dangerous animals can still stick their noses or antlers through the wires and possibly injure someone standing too close. This bull elk in "rut", for instance, can become extremely aggressive and dangerous at this time of year and will often "charge" at people standing too near the fence.

PASTURES

AWCC plants 25 acres of annual cereal rye for the elk and bison herds every spring. All the grasses and fertilizer selected is done via USDA and NRCS programs.

Mike Miller, Executive Director of AWCC, plants and fertilizes some of the pastures during the spring. These nutritious grasses (along with the natural grasses and other foods) will sustain the "browsers and grazers" such as the elk, bison, moose, muskoxen, deer, and caribou. Also, since these various animals eat the grasses differently, it is necessary to rotate them occasionally to best utilize the food source.

During the winter months, the animals (such as this bull elk) are provided fresh hay to rest on when staying outside their shelters.

Below: A herd of elk graze on the newly sprouting grass.

1964 EARTHQUAKE

Earthquake damaged building along Seward highway.

On March 27, 1964, the strongest earthquake to hit North America in recorded history struck Alaska. A 9.2 on the Richter Scale, seismic motion at Portage was violent and lasted over 6 minutes. Ground fissures and shaking damaged buildings, the highway, and the railroad. Also, the ground dropped 8 feet in some areas.

Once a busy little town, Portage was abandoned, leaving a ghost town among the skeleton trees.

AWCC's caribou rest beside another damaged building.

Moose standing in extreme high-tide water.

The land that AWCC occupies today was above high-tide prior to the 1964 earthquake. Since then, the subsided grounds is flooded by seawater during extreme high-tides. This has killed the cottonwood and spruce trees, turning forest into wetlands. These standing dead trees are very evident here.

The land is on the rise again, and slowly the forest plants will reappear. In the meanwhile, certain pastures at AWCC will temporarily hold water until the high-tide recedes, giving the residing animals some water to splash around in and enjoy.

Grizzly

A young photographer snaps a picture of Sitka Black-tailed deer.

Malissa Casto, AWCC Director of Operations, with new Black bear friend. Photo by Calvin Hall.

Staff members and volunteers of AWCC dedicate their time and effort to tirelessly care for the wild, injured, orphaned or relocated animals that are brought to the Center. As with most similar wildlife-care facilities, AWCC is usually unable to return these same animals back into the wild, due to the animals having become accustomed to the care received and to their caretakers. Birds, however, (if not too injured) are sometimes released due to their more independent nature.

Sitka black-tailed deer fawn

Coyote pup

Moose calves

During the winter ski-season, "Chugach Powder Guides" of Girdwood uses the property edge of AWCC to load up skiers that wish to be flown to remote areas in search of fresh "powder".

Moose biologist, Dr. Vic Van Ballenberghe, feeding a banana to Seymour the moose and checking on its health. **<u>PLEASE</u>** do not try this with a wild moose as they can be *very dangerous* and unpredictable.

Although most bison calves are born in the spring/summer months, "Ice cube" (far left) was born in January, 2006 to "Sugar".

This photograph shows a herd of Plains bison on a cold (below zero) January day in 2006. The bison herds are often moved to AWCC's various pastures and allowed to browse on the natural vegetation growing there. Also, it shows some of the high mountains that surround the Alaska Wildlife Conservation Center's property.

A young visitor gets a close-up view of a magnificent grizzly. AWCC's bears will normally go into their dens and hibernate during the winter months but will sometimes come out during periods of warm weather. The bears seem as interested in "us" as we are in "them" and seem to enjoy *people-watching*.

There is, incidentally, about a three-foot spread between the two sets of fences that separate the bears and their viewers. *DO NOT* climb over the first fence!

Wild eagles are seen most everyday here at AWCC. They have become accustomed to seeing people and will often perch near the lodge/gift shop.

Here a wild Bald eagle has landed on the fence outside Adonis's enclosure. This common occurrence is probably due either to the sight of food inside the captive eagle's cage or the wild eagle may identify Adonis as a possible mate.

The Bald eagle is America's national bird and is a "protected" species. However, despite this protection and their value to nature, they are still often shot by humans.

Although "stressed" upon arrival, the animals (such as this deer fawn) quickly adapt to their caretakers.

18

Young visitors enjoy watching a newly-arrived orphaned fawn.

Hopefully you brought your camera with! AWCC is a great place to get wildlife photographs like of this magnificent bull elk.

Visitors from Texas run along the fence line with Hugo the grizzly.

Two young girls going nose-to-nose with a bull moose.

Watching the AWCC staff and volunteers bottle-feed the orphaned or injured baby animals (such as these moose calves) is an enjoyable experience for visitors. The calves or fawns somewhat aggressive feeding style will certainly make you smile or laugh.

Feeding times are posted at the lodge.

The Black bear cub (opposite page) was brought to AWCC as an orphan and, after it had become accustomed and fond of people, was housed in a fenced-in area outside the lodge so it could be monitored.

Sitka Black-tailed deer fawn

Top: Immature lynx. Photo by Gary Lackie.   Bottom: Black bear cub.

The building shown below is the "Bio Fact Barn", a building that houses an incredible amount of information and hands-on activities as well as assorted artifacts such as antlers, bear claws, furs, skulls and feathers. Also, videos are available to watch for those visitors with plenty of time.

The Bio Fact Barn and its staff will help provide visitors with wildlife awareness and education. Please stop by if you have any questions.

In 2005, AWCC was given a grant by the State of Alaska, Division of Agriculture, to produce a garden of Alaska Grown vegetables. This produce will be used to feed the AWCC's animals and also to educate visitors about the Alaska Grown program and teach them the importance of the agricultural industry in Alaska.

This project could not have been completed without the generous donations of Alaska Mill and Feed, Anchor Point Greenhouse, the Rempel Family Farm, AWCC volunteer Jeri Skille as well as many other volunteers, staff and interns.

AWCC's "Alaska Grown" garden.

Lupine

Spruce tree in January

Fireweed

Autumn leaves

THE "SEASONS" AT AWCC

Spring: Look for new arrivals in the spring at AWCC. Some animals may be born here, such as bison (April-May), elk (May-July), and muskox (May-June). Many orphaned and injured animals are brought to the center for treatment during the spring and summer months.

Summer: This is the time of year when adult animals must regain the strength and weight that harsh Alaska winters normally make them lose. Young animals grow rapidly during this "endless daylight" period.

Autumn: This is the season of the "rut" when large mammals mate and fighting amongst males occurs. Here at AWCC the males of the aggressive species are separated in order to selectively breed the females and also to prevent injuries to the combatants.

Winter: In Alaska's wilds, only the hardiest and most adaptable birds and mammals survive this unforgiving season. The resident animals of AWCC do not suffer this natural hardship and instead enjoy food and shelter daily.

A summer flower patch near AWCC's entrance.

AWCC is open everyday and some visitors (especially Alaska residents that live nearby) are fortunate enough to visit the facilities and the resident animals throughout the year. They, along with artists and photographers, are able to watch and "shoot" these wildlife creatures in all the varied seasons of the year. No one season seems to be "better" than any other and it is fun to watch the newborns of spring grow and play throughout the year.

Because of the longer summer daylight hours, Alaska Wildlife Conservation Center is open longer hours than it is during the shorter daylight hours of the winter months.

<u>Spring</u>. Muskox cow (shedding its "qiviut") and calf.

<u>Summer.</u> "Hugo", AWCC's first grizzly bear, plays with a favorite toy.

Photo by Gary Lackie (glackie@gci.net)

<u>Autumn</u>. On a frosty autumn morning, a large bull elk "bugles".

<u>Winter</u>. A bull caribou still carries his antlers but will shed them soon.

WILDLIFE OF ALASKA WILDLIFE CONSERVATION CENTER

Wild birds, such as this Bald eagle, are frequent visitors to AWCC and are often seen perched high in the trees. Some of the eagles, as well as many magpies, ravens, and owls, spend the entire year in Alaska and do not migrate south. They are efficient scavengers and often steal food from AWCC's resident animals.

Other owls, such as this Northern Hawk owl, patrol the Portage valley area seeking prey birds and small mammals.

The deadly talons of hawks, owls and eagles make these birds efficient predators.

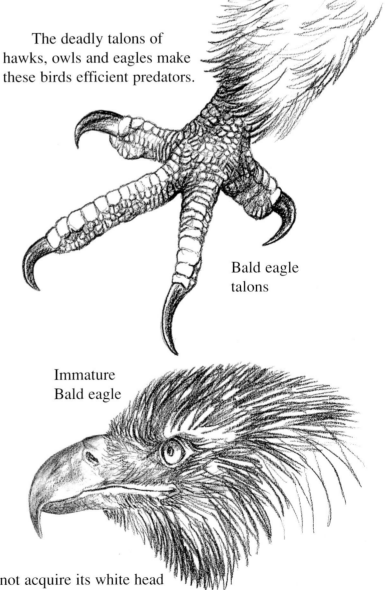

Bald eagle talons

This Great-horned owl was a victim of gunshot wounds and suffered severe wing injuries. It has been a resident at AWCC since 1999.

Immature Bald eagle

Adonis (having a "bad hair day" in the wind) was also a gunshot victim and required a wing amputation.

A Bald eagle does not acquire its white head and tail until it is over 4 years old.

Photo by Calvin Hall

This female Red-tailed hawk was trained as a passage bird by Malissa Casto under a federal falconry permit. Malissa used this hawk as an educational bird and gave programs to AWCC visitors, schools, and the Begich Boggs Visitor Center. After two years of captivity this bird was released into the wild.

Programs such as these will help educate many young people, teaching them to respect and protect these important and magnificent wild creatures.
** The Red-tailed hawk is a large bird with a four foot wingspan. Its "keeeer" scream is heard throughout most of North America.

Rufous Hummingbird: These beautiful males are distinguished from all other birds by its unique coloration; especially its flaming reddish-orange throat patch. Hummingbirds are able to flap their wings over 70 times per second and are the only birds known to fly backwards. AWCC maintains hummingbird feeders near its lodge during the spring and summer months. Both photos by Calvin Hall (www.alaskasaurora.com)

Lesser Yellowlegs

Wilson's Snipe

Trumpeter swans fly over AWCC in October on their migration south. Usually they'll stay here in southcentral Alaska until all the feeding ponds and marshes are frozen.

Raven. This large, black bird is a very aggressive scavenger, and is commonly seen throughout the Portage valley.

Swans swimming in the waters boarding AWCC.

Canada geese are one of the first signs of spring for many Alaskans. They normally come into the southcentral area of Alaska in mid-April and then migrate back south in October. Their raucous "honks" are a welcome sound.

Wildlife incentive ponds at AWCC provide refuge and a release site for recuperating waterfowl.

Black-billed magpies are the most commonly seen birds here at AWCC. Their intelligence and persistence allows them to ignore nearby humans and sweep in to steal food (such as dog food pellets and meat and fish scraps) from the resident animals.

Ducks, such as these Mallard drakes, often visit the many AWCC ponds during the warmer months of the year.

A dominant coyote enjoys a snack while a more submissive coyote and a pair of magpies await any leftovers.

Porcupine quills. Quills are not "thrown", as often thought, but rather are imbedded in a predator by the porcupine's flicking of its tail.

"Needles" the porcupine was brought to AWCC in 2001 after it and its mother (who did not survive) were hit by a car. Needles suffered neurological damage and has become a permanent resident.

Ermine, like Alaska's Snowshoe hares, also turn white to match their winter environment. This camouflage helps both the predator (ermine) and prey (hare) hide.

Small Mammals

A Snowshoe hare's large back "snowshoe type" feet will help it when running across snow covered terrain.

Snowshoe hare / summer coat

Snowshoe hare / winter coat

KIT
June

Red Fox

Young Red fox curls up to sleep.

The Red fox is common throughout most of Alaska and has acquired a well deserved reputation as being a sly and cunning creature.

An adult fox will measure up to 32" in length and sport a 16" bushy tail. Adults will weigh from 6 to 15 pounds, even though it appears heavier when seen in its thick winter coat. Male Red fox are called "dogs" and the females are called "vixens".

Red fox in snowstorm. AWCC photo by Gary Lackie.

Red fox kit

"Daisy" (and her litter-mates) were brought to AWCC due to their den being located too near an active airplane runway. This *dangerous location* was deemed unacceptable and resulted in the fox families relocation. Photo by Calvin Hall.

A Red fox and grizzly bear seem to be sizing each other up here in their AWCC enclosure. Although fox are wary and quick, grizzlies are able to reach full speed in very short order, and so the enclosure's fox and coyotes must be very careful and not approach too close.

The Red fox, incidentally, is not always "red" and has distinct color phases. They are: red, cross, silver, and black. Shades of red, however, are the most common coloration.

"Kits" are born in April/May and are able to hunt when about 3 months old. Family groups break up in autumn and each animal strikes out on its own.

Coyote

Here at AWCC, visitors are able to watch the resident animals interact with one another and also watch as residents (such as this coyote) interact with wild, visiting animals (such as this Black-billed magpie).

Coyote in patch of lupine.

Coyote in lush, warm autunm coat.

Coyote in "ratty" summer coat.

Alaska's coyotes are often mistaken for wolves as they have a somewhat similar look. They are, however, less than half as large. A coyote's distinctive features include a sharply pointed nose, sharply pointed ears (that never droop) and a long bushy tail.

Coyote / autumn

Coyotes normally weigh 20 to 30 pounds, stand 24" at their shoulder, and (including tail) are 48" long. They are mostly grayish in color and normally have a black-tipped tail. Their yipping-yapping howl is often heard at AWCC, especially when a distant train blows its whistle.

Young coyote pup / summer

Pup study

This alert coyote keeps a sharp eye out for the grizzly bears that he and his family share this large 18- acre enclosure with. Or, is it watching for the "feed-wagon" to arrive? The enclosure's numerous log piles are frequently used as look-outs by these coyotes and bears as well as visiting ravens, magpies, and Bald eagles.

Lynx

The lynx is Alaska's only native cat. It is a long-legged, large-footed, short-tailed, buffy gray colored cat that has long tufts on the tips of its ears and heavy cheek ruffs.

A mature lynx weighs from 20 to 35 pounds and measures about 30" to 40" from the tip of its nose to the end of its black-tipped tail.

These lynx kittens were burned in a forest fire in July and were brought to AWCC for healing and recuperation. They are being temporarily held at another location until a habitat is constructed at AWCC.

Yawning lynx (note the large paws)

Lynx kittens are normally born in May/June and will stay with their mother until the following March or April mating season, after which they will then all go their separate ways. When prey is abundant (especially hares) the lynx will have a high survival rate. When prey is scarce, however, very few yearlings breed and very few kittens survive through the following winter.

Their very large paws help them move swiftly across the winter's snow covered terrain in pursuit of their prey.

Snowshoe hares, like this one shown in summer coat, are an important prey animal for the lynx.

Lynx photos by Gary Lackie

The caribou at AWCC were rescued from Alaskan islands, which were becoming over-populated and could not sustain healthy animals. To prevent starvation, some caribou were removed and brought to AWCC.

All caribou and the domesticated reindeer are considered to be the same species. Alaska's only wild caribou subspecies is the barren ground caribou.

Caribou

Caribou calf

Calves average 13 pounds at birth and may double their weight within two weeks.

Caribou are members of the deer family and are the only member whose females grow antlers. The antlers of the males (bulls), however, are much larger than those of the females (cows). Also, the cows retain their antlers until their calves are born in May or June, and the bulls drop theirs after the autumn "rut".

Mature bulls will average 300 to 400 pounds in weight and cows will weigh around 200 pounds. Alaska's most northern caribou will often weigh less than those from Alaska's south or Interior.

Caribou are "migraters" and must be constantly on the move in order to find adequate food.

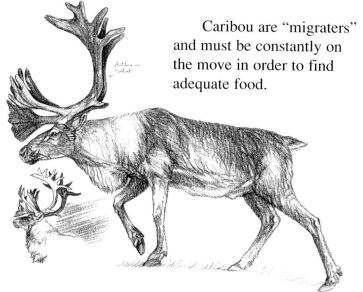

Antlers are a form of growing bone and as they grow during the year they are sheathed in a blood-nourished skin often called "velvet". Once the antlers are full grown, the velvet is shed, exposing the bone antlers beneath.

Bull caribou

Caribou calves are able to run and keep up with their mother (and herd) within a day or two of birth.

Antlers are shed after the bull caribou's annual "rut" and it is common to see the animals keep one antler for a few days after the other one has shed.

The males of the deer family all sport antlers which are used to fight with against competing bulls during the yearly autumn mating season. Their shapes are such that they make effective weapons (against predators such as wolves too) as well as effectively protecting their eyes from most injuries.

Caribou have large, concave hoofs that spread apart widely to support the heavy animal as it walks across snow or spongy tundra. These wide hooves also make good paddles when they swim across rivers or lakes.

Mature bull caribou / autumn

Calves begin taking solid food within a few days of birth.

Alaska Moose

Alaska's moose are the world's largest members of the deer family and a mature male (bull) can weigh up to 1600 pounds and stand 6 feet high at the shoulder. Females (cows) normally weigh from 800 to 1200 pounds. Calves are about 30 pounds at birth.

Moose calves await their upcoming bottle-feeding.

Two bull moose in a late November snow-storm. Although the large mammals here at AWCC do have shelters to protect them from the elements, the hardy species are quite able to thrive throughout the long, cold Alaskan winters

Bull moose antler shedding its "velvet". This shedding occurs in the autumn just prior to the moose's annual "rut" and exposes the hard, fighting-ready antlers.

Two bull moose sparring.

This rear view of a moose's antler shows the grooves where blood vessels supplied the nourishment to the growing antler when it was still sheathed in velvet.

<u>BULL MOOSE</u>. The Alaska moose is the largest moose in the world.

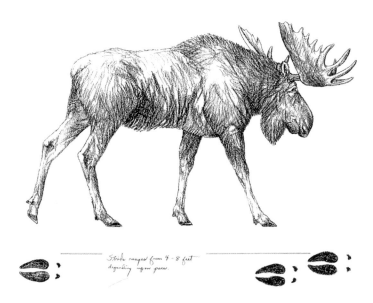

In 2005, AWCC had four bull moose: Seymour, Chimo, River, and Vic. Since breeding moose is not an objective of the Center, the incoming female moose are normally transferred after they have been healed or grown sufficiently. This lessens the problems that may arise due to fighting and subsequent injuries that may otherwise occur during the annual "rut".

The dewlap (or "bell') hanging beneath a mooses chin will vary in shape and its purpose is unknown.

Bull moose eating a Halloween pumpkin.

Seymour (the moose shown on previous page) was an orphaned calf that wandered into a yard in Hunter Creek, Alaska in 1996. AWCC has been his home since 1997 and he is probably the world's most "famous" moose due to his many commercials, nature shows and movies.

Rocky Mountain Elk

Elk calves are born between May and July and weigh between 25 and 40 pounds. They will grow rapidly on their mother's rich milk and will lose their "spotted" camouflaged coat in about three months.

Elk are one of the larger members of the deer family and the mature bulls will often weigh over a 1000 pounds and sport antlers that are 5 feet long. In Alaska, the wild elk are restricted to some of the islands of the Southeast. Elk are also called "wapiti".

Rocky Mountain elk calves in July.

Photo by Gary Lackie

This unique photo of a bugling bull elk shows its upper two ivory teeth. In the 19th century, thousands of elk were killed solely for these two teeth, which were popular as watch-fob charms. Of course, ranchers often killed many additional thousands of elk because they competed with their livestock for food.

A bull elk (in "rut") displaying his aggressive mood.

Bull elk in beginning annual antler growth.

In nature, young animals are sometimes born late in the season. These animals, especially in the North, often perish due to their inability to cope with the winter's deep snows, cold temperatures and food availability. Here at AWCC, however, these "late bloomers" are protected from these hazards and thrive.

Nursing calf / August

Like the Plains bison, many of the elk at AWCC were once ranch animals. A breeding herd of these Rocky Mountain elk are maintained here and the mating is carefully monitored in order to produce the healthiest offspring.

Cow elk are VERY protective and maintain a close relationship with their calves for many months. Calves may suckle for up to nine months after birth. One or two calves will be born from May to July to mature, healthy cows.

To become a dominant breeding bull, a bull must firstly defeat the area's other competing bulls.

Elk are very gregarious and cow/calf herds are usually separate from the nearby bull herds until the annual autumn mating season. Than the dominant bull will control and breed a harem of cows, often announcing his status and location via a melodious and eerie "bugle".

Maintaining a large herd of cows is usually a full-time job for the dominant bull elk, and he often enters the long, harsh winters in a state of malnourishment and possible injury from his many fights. Here at AWCC the bulls are separated during the peak of the "rut" and only a selected bull is allowed to breed.

Fawns are normally born in May and June and weigh 6 to 8 pounds.

Sitka Black-tailed Deer

Twin fawns hide in the tall grasses and brush until called by their mother for nursing.

The Sitka Black-tailed deer are surely the "friendliest" animals here at AWCC. They seem to love being near people and are very easy to feed and care for.

Mothers identify their young by smell.

Mature does in their prime years (5 to 10 years) will usually produce two fawns yearly. In the wild, deer will live to about 15. Naturally, as with many wild creatures, severe winters, predators, and diminished habitat will limit deer populations.

Week old "spotted" fawn

Twin fawns nursing / July

Antlers of "sitkas" are relatively small in size as compared to other deer species. A normal antler configuration is three points on each side (including the eyeguard).

Sitka Black-tailed deer are distinguished by their short face and very noticeable blackish colored tails.

Antler configuration will vary according to heredity and nutrition availability. Also, as shown on the mature buck below, antlers may sometimes be deformed due to an injury during the antler's annual formation.

The Sitka Black-tailed deer is a smaller and stockier deer than the other members of the Black-tailed group. A mature female (doe) will weigh about 80 pounds and males (bucks) will weigh 120 to 150 pounds on average.

The deer's summer coat is usually a reddish-brown coloration, and its winter coat is more of a grayish-brown color.

Buck

The Wood Bison Project

The Wood bison at AWCC are part of a state recovery program planned by the Alaska Department of Fish and Game which hopes to reintroduce the endangered subspecies back to Alaska's wilds. Wood bison were once present in Alaska but were totally eliminated (mainly due to hunting) in the early 1900's.

The bison at AWCC arrived in November, 2003 from the Yukon Territory of Canada. Six males and seven females were the beginning herd and a few calves have since been born. The bison will stay at AWCC for a couple of years, to develop a stable herd size and prepare them for release. While residing here the herd of bison have a large 50 acre enclosure to range and browse in.

This calf is the first Wood bison calf born in Alaska in over 100 years. Photo: June, 2005

The Wood bison is the northern cousin of the Plains bison that roams many states down-below. It is bigger than the Plains bison and a large, mature bull will often weigh 2,250 pounds versus the 1,900 pounds of the smaller Plains. A mature cow will weigh about 1,000 pounds.

Calves are born from May to July and are a reddish color for a few weeks. They begin to grow horns and develop a bison's "hump" at about two months.

Wood Bison

Calf

Cow

Bull

Wood bison
calves

Newborn calves stay near their mothers during their first few weeks.

The Wood bison at AWCC have a large 50-acre enclosure to roam around in, which allows them plenty of natural browse and grasses as well as providing the "privacy" needed by the cows to give birth away from the main herd.

A bison's large, cloven-heart shaped hooves will leave tracks that are similar to a domestic cow's tracks.

There are several characteristics that distinguish Wood bison and Plains bison. Wood bison are slightly heavier, taller, have a higher and squarer hump, and have little or no chap hair on their forelegs. Wood bison also have long, straighter hair on their head and a smaller chin beard.

Top: Wood bison bull   **Bottom: Plains bison bull**

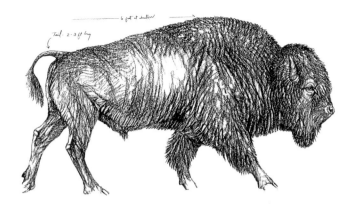

Plains Bison

Bull in December snowstorm.

Mothers, such as this Plains bison cow, are extremely protective of their newborn calves.

There are a number of wild herds of Plains bison roaming in Alaska now, due to past transplantations from "outside" sources. These herds appear to be healthy and expanding and a limited hunting lottery is usually held yearly.

"Ice cube" and "Sugar"

The Plains bison is only slightly smaller than the more northern Wood bison, which is the largest terrestrial animal in North America. They are dark brown with "humped" shoulders, shaggy manes and beards. Both the male (bull) and female (cow) have short, sharply-pointed horns. Commonly called "buffalo" by most people, although it is not a true buffalo. AWCC's Plains bison were acquired from a ranch with excess animals.

LEFT: "Ice cube" was born in -20 degree weather in January of 2006. This "very unusual" winter birth (bison calves are usually born during the spring/summer months) earned him this fitting nickname.

Plains bison bull. A Black-billed magpie is gathering loose hairs for its nest and/or searching for insects.

Muskox

The muskox, as a species, has changed little since the Ice age and is an animal perfectly suited for its harsh arctic environment. It is called "omingmak" by the Inupiaq-speaking Eskimos, referring to its long hair that hangs almost to the ground.

Mature bull muskox are about 5 feet high at the shoulder and weigh up to 800 pounds. Cows stand about 4 feet tall and weigh up to 500 pounds. Single calves are born in the spring (April to June) and weigh 20 to 30 pounds. They grow rapidly and often weigh over 200 pounds as yearlings.

The original Alaska muskoxen were eliminated in the 1800's, due mostly to overhunting. A transplantation from Greenland established a small herd on Nunivak Island and from which further transplantations have occurred. The return of the animals to Alaska has been an important success story in wildlife conservation.

Muskox cows and calves in early summer. Note the shedding "qiviut" on the cows.

Bull

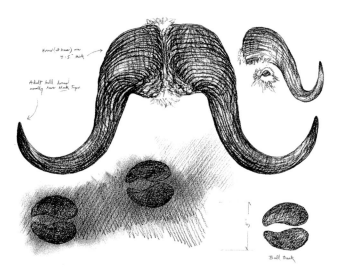

Both cows and bulls have horns, but the bull's horns are heavier and larger.

During the mating season the battles between competing bulls are awesome and violent. Two bulls will rush each other and crash horns with a force that has been measured to equal a car running into a concrete wall at 20 mph. Luckily the bulls heavily armored skulls protect them from harm.

During the summer, the muskox will shed their wool-like underhair (called "qiviut"). It has been called the world's rarest fiber and is spun by Natives and others to produce warm, soft and valuable garments.

Charging bull! Be careful near fences.

2005 was the first year that muskox calves were born at the Alaska Wildlife Conservation Center.

Muskoxen are a dark brownish color with lighter creamy colored hair on their legs, face, and "saddle". All four cloven hooves are the same size.

Family portrait. A cow and bull seemingly guard their young calf.

Black bears weigh under a pound and are mostly hairless when born in their mother's winter den. They continue to nurse on the sow's rich milk until they emerge from their den in late spring. Black bears often produce one litter of cubs every other year when conditions are ideal. Sows usually firstly mate in their third year and, at maturity, will commonly bear two cubs.

Black Bears

Black bear cub.

Adult

Black bears are the smallest of the North American bears. A mature adult will stand about 29" at the shoulders and measure about 60" from nose to tail. In Alaska, a mature male seldom weighs over 250 pounds.

Black bears are not always "black", and their colors range from white to brown to jet black. They can be distinguished from grizzly bears by their less pronounced shoulder hump, straight facial profile and their short, sharply curved claws. As with grizzlies/Brown bears, Black bears spend the winter months in hibernation. Pregnant females will give birth to cubs (two is most common) in this winter den. These cubs are born blind, nearly hairless, and weigh under a pound.

Because of their claw configuration and their lighter weights, Black bears are able to climb trees throughout their lives.

Black bears are called the "All-American bear", because it is only found in North America.

Two Black bears, Kuma and Uli, often perch in one of their favorite trees to sleep. Kuma arrived at AWCC in May, 2002 weighing only three pounds. He arrived only one week before Uli arrived at the Center. She was found wandering the streets of Juneau alone. They have since become inseparable "best friends".

This "bears in a tree" scene is one of the most photographed scenes here at AWCC.

Black bears lack the grizzlie's pronounced shoulder "hump".

Kuma and Uli

AWCC normally receives orphaned or injured bear cubs every year and is able to ship them to other facilities after they have been restored to full health.

However, zoos and wildlife parks often have all the bears needed, and "placing" these animals in proper environments has become more and more difficult.

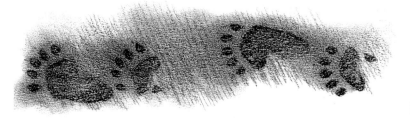

North America has three species of bears – the Black bear, the Grizzly bear, and the Polar bear. Here at AWCC, only the Black bears and Grizzly bears are current residents.

Ears "laid back" is a sign that a bear is stressed and may charge.

Black bear cubs / June. Photo: Calvin Hall.

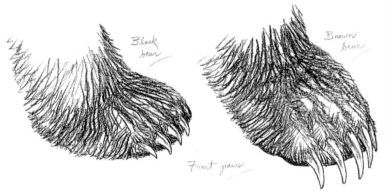

Black bear cub / July

Bears stand on their back legs in order to see, hear or smell better. They cannot, however, run on these back legs.

Adult Black bear / June

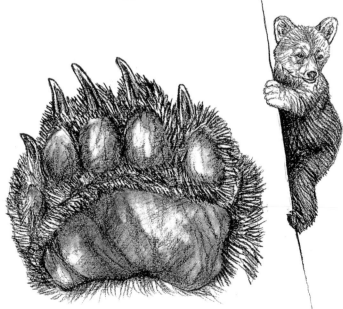

Female

Grizzly cubs, like Black bear cubs, are born in their mother's winter den sometime between January and March and weigh about a pound. Litter sizes range from one to four, but two is the most common. These cubs will remain with their mother for at least two-and-one half years, indicating that the sow will not breed for at least three years.

Grizzly Bear

An adult "Hugo" in a winter snowstorm.

"Hugo" was a great tree climber as a cub.

The Grizzly bear and Brown bear are actually the same species. The name "Brown bear" is often used to describe bears living in the southern coastal regions of Alaska and the name "Grizzly bear" is used to describe this specie of bear that lives inland from the coast. Kodiak Island Brown bears are usually considered a separate subspecies due to their isolation from the mainland populations of bears. They are also considered the largest Brown bears and weigh up to 1600 pounds.

A log leaned up against the backside of the Grizzly bear's little log cabin allows them access to the roof where, at times, meat or fish scraps are thrown. This elevated view gives AWCC's visitors many good photos.

The Grizzly bear has a sturdy, densely furred body; small rounded ears and a concave (dish-shaped) face. They possess a large muscular "hump" atop their shoulders and have long, slightly-curved claws. They can range in color from whitish to black and an individuals may change throughout the year due to sun bleaching and molting.

Grizzly/Brown bears have been known to live over 30 years in the wild, but mid-20's is more average. Their sense of smell is exceptional and their sight and hearing are comparable to that of humans.

Checking the roof for possible snacks.

Grizzly tracks

Bears are exceptional athletes and can pull themselves up with their front legs and can stand on their hind legs to help them reach high.

Also, do not think you can outrun a Grizzly bear, as they are said to be able to out-race a racehorse (from a dead start) for a quarter-mile.

Grizzlies are amongst the most playful of large mammals and, when not playing with other bears, will often grab a stick or rock or antler to toss and drag around. Also, balls are a favorite toy in their big swimming hole.

Sometimes you just get "played out" and crawl up a tree to grab a needed snooze.

Hugo is a female grizzly from Hugo Mountain near Kotzebue, Alaska. Two men riding snow machines found her in November, 2000. She had hundreds of porcupine quills imbedded in her paws. Severely dehydrated and malnourished, Hugo was unable to walk or eat when brought to AWCC. Hugo was the first bear to receive a permanent home at AWCC.

Cubs / August

Antlers are a great source of calcium and are usually chewed-up by rodents and other mammals. Since antlers are shed yearly by members of the deer family (Moose, Elk, Caribou, Deer), they are constantly replenished.

Joe Boxer and Patron arrived at AWCC in 2002 after their mother was killed "in defense of property" near Willow, Alaska. Their unusual names are the result of a fund-raiser held jointly for Dream Foundation and AWCC. An auction was held in which the winner got to choose names for the orphaned bears. The successful bidders were executives from the clothing brand JOE BOXER and Patron Spirits. The names were chosen in honor of their companies.

Joe Boxer and Patron *people-watching* from atop a log pile in 2005.

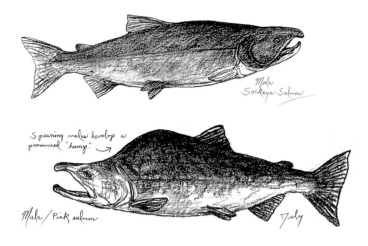

Male
Sockeye Salmon

Spawning males develop a
pronounced "hump"

Male / Pink salmon   July

The bears that live on the coast line and have access to the year's salmon runs will be able to "fatten-up" prior to the annual hibernation. This rich food source will allow the bears to add from 25 to 70% to their body weight and allow them to survive the long winters without additional food. Going into their den in good condition will also ensure that the females will bear and raise healthy cubs.

Since Hugo had spent much of her first years alone, she was very reluctant to get too near Joe Boxer and Patron when they were introduced into her large enclosure in the summer of 2005. Whenever they would approach her, she would flee and then often stand on her back legs at a distance to see if they were still following.

After a few weeks, however, the bears gradually adjusted to each others presence and now are often seen playing and resting together. Although the "cubs" are about 2 years younger than Hugo, they will soon be larger in size and may therefore choose to be more dominant in nature.

LEFT: After Halloween, the AWCC animals are often given leftover pumpkins to eat from local stores. The bears, elk, moose, deer, bison, and muskox all seem to enjoy this seasonal treat.

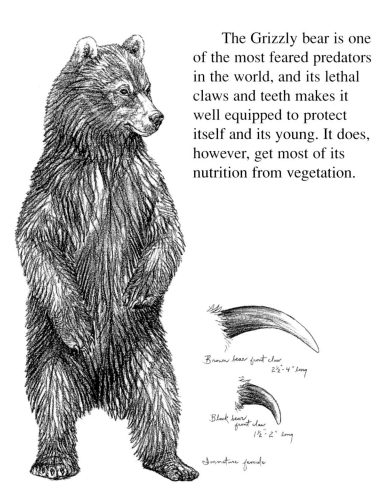

The Grizzly bear is one of the most feared predators in the world, and its lethal claws and teeth makes it well equipped to protect itself and its young. It does, however, get most of its nutrition from vegetation.

Brown bear front claw
2½"- 4" long

Black bear front claw
1½"- 2" long

Immature female

SOW
3 - 3½ ft at shoulder

Although this above sketch is of an immature female bear, a large Kodiak bear can stand over 9 feet tall.

Grizzlies play-fighting.

The front claws of a Grizzly bear may be 4" long, hence aiding their digging up rodents and vegetation.

Alaska Wildlife Conservation Center <u>thanks you</u>
for your support; either through your admission fees,
gift shop purchases, donations or membership.

Muskox cow and calf in early May.

All proceeds from this non-profit organization
are dedicated to the wild animals in our care and
AWCC's education programs.